MINUTE
MOTIVATORS

Instant Insights for Leaders

STAN TOLER

Beacon Hill Press of Kansas City
Kansas City, Missouri

Copyright 1996
by Beacon Hill Press of Kansas City
ISBN 083-411-6340

Printed in the
United States of America

Cover Design: Ted Ferguson

10   9   8   7   6   5   4   3   2   1

To my wife, Linda, who during our 23 years of marriage has modeled leadership excellence in our home with our two sons, Seth and Adam. I love you!

Stan

ontents

Special Thanks

To the Beacon Hill Press of Kansas City leadership team—Bob Brower and Michael Estep —for their guidance and oversight of this project. Additionally, and more importantly, thanks for Christian friendship and all the good fellowship involved in preparation for this project.

To Michael Johnson, Derl Keefer, and Jim Williams for creative insight, research, and editorial assistance. You guys are terrific!

*I*ntroduction

"Growing" leaders has never been an easy assignment. In this book, *Minute Motivators*, I have shared concise, easy-to-read principles for effective leadership.

The concept and design of this book should help leaders in any sphere of influence, whether it's in the marketplace or in the church. It is my prayer that these shared thoughts will help you in your quest to grow and develop as a leader.

STAN TOLER
EPHESIANS 3:20-21

LESSONS
FROM LEADERS

---

*G*rowing leaders
rub shoulders
with great leaders.

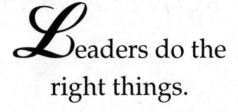

*L*eaders do the
right things.

WARREN BENNIS

*L*eadership is leaders inducing followers to act for certain goals that represent the values and motivations, the wants and needs, the aspirations and expectations of both leaders and followers. And the genius of leadership lies in the manner in which leaders see and act on their own and their followers' values and motivations.

JAMES McGREGOR BURNS

*M*ost people do not know what they can do because all they're told is what they cannot do.

ZIG ZIGLAR

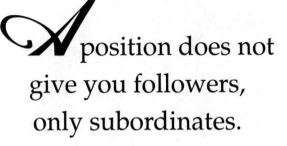

A position does not give you followers, only subordinates.

JOHN GARDNER

*L*eadership is the ability to organize the spiritual gifts and limitations of others.

J. OSWALD SANDERS

*D*elegate
responsibility and
ownership by
empowering people to
act on their own.

DONALD T. PHILLIPS

*W*here success is concerned, people are not measured in inches or pounds, or college degrees, or family background. They are measured by the size of their thinking. How big we think determines the size of our accomplishments.

DAVID SCHWARTZ

I use not only the
brains I have,
but all I can borrow.

WOODROW WILSON

*T*he way you see your future determines your thinking today, and your thinking today determines your performance today.

ANTHONY CAMPOLO

*T*o manage is
to control. To lead
is to liberate.

HARRISON OWEN

*I*nnovative leaders
have a clear agenda,
purpose, and focus
on results.

WARREN BENNIS

That which holds
one's attention
determines one's
actions.

*T*he really great leader is the one who makes everyone feel worthwhile.

*I*t is a never-ending task to become an effective leader, because time changes all things. Therefore, you must discipline yourself to keep up with change.

A fundamental challenge leaders face is how to translate their values and purpose into practice, while operating in a rapidly changing environment.

WILLIAM B. JOINER

*I*n every organized
event there has been
a bold leader, an object
or purpose, or an
adversary.

FRED SMITH

*S*imply and plainly defined, a leader is a person who has followers.

WILFERD PETERSON

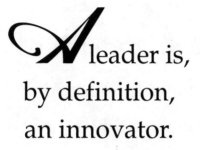

A leader is,
by definition,
an innovator.

WARREN BENNIS

*L*eadership is:

♦ knowing what to do next,

♦ knowing why it's important,

♦ knowing how to bring appropriate resources to bear on the need at hand.

BOBB BIEHL

*I*f a man is called to be a street sweeper, he should sweep streets even as Michelangelo painted, or Beethoven composed music, or Shakespeare wrote poetry. He should sweep streets so well that all the hosts of heaven and earth will pause to say, "Here lived a great street sweeper who did his job well."

MARTIN LUTHER KING JR.

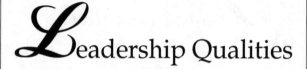

*L*eadership Qualities

♦ *Visionary* toward the future

♦ *Integrity* in lifestyle

♦ *Grows* other leaders

♦ *Places Confidence* in teammates

♦ *Networks* with other leaders

♦ *Connects* with people

♦ *Is Willing* to take risks

LEADERS ARE VISIONARIES

---

*T*he very essence of leadership is that you have a vision.

THEODORE HESBURGH

A leader is one who sees *more* than others see, who sees *farther* than others see, and who sees *before* others do.

LeROY EIMS

*T*he first responsibility of a leader is to define reality.

MAX DuPREE, *Leadership Is an Art*

*V*ision is the spirit
behind an organization.

DONALD H. KUHN

Great leaders inspire us to go places we would never go on our own, and to attempt things we never thought we had in us.

HANS FINZEL,
Top Ten Mistakes Leaders Make

*T*o grasp and hold a vision—that is the essence of successful leadership.

RONALD REAGAN

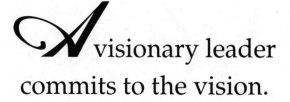

A visionary leader commits to the vision.

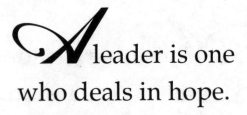

A leader is one
who deals in hope.

NAPOLÉON BONAPARTE

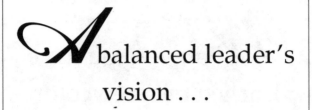

A balanced leader's vision . . .

is liberating.

is a compass.

is lifelong.

is a life and death issue.

must be shared.

WILLIAM EASUM

*W*hatever you have learned or received or heard from me, or seen in me—put it into practice. And the God of peace will be with you *(Phil. 4:9)*.

LEADERS ARE INFLUENCERS

---

*L*eadership is
influence!

JOHN C. MAXWELL

*I*nspirational in style.

*N*ever-failing in promises.

*F*orgives quickly.

*L*oves God.

*U*nderstands people.

*E*ncourages others with praise.

*N*ever quits.

*C*ommunicates the vision.

*E*nthusiastic about the future.

LEADERS ARE COMMUNICATORS

*T*he greatest illusion
of communication is that
it has been achieved.

GEORGE BERNARD SHAW

*S*uccessful leaders communicate well. They:

express thoughts with confidence.

research the topic thoroughly.

share "take-away" principles effectively.

use humor to keep the crowd alert.

understand their audience.

speak with clarity.

are concise with their presentation.

LEADERS ARE POSITIVE

---

*P*ositive thinking
without positive faith
will result in
positive failure.

Achiever's Creed

Whatever the mind can
conceive,
And I will dare to
believe,
With God's help,
I will achieve.

DALE GALLOWAY

LEADERS ARE LEARNERS

---

*A*ll leaders are learners. The moment you stop learning, you stop leading.

RICK WARREN

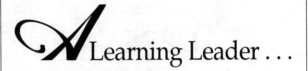

A Learning Leader . . .

builds a relationship with other leaders.

understands the power of fellowship.

shares responsibility with others.

seeks the collective wisdom of the team.

accepts pain and disappointment in stride.

never stops reading.

attends conferences and seminars.

shares success with the team.

*I*f the ax is dull and its edge unsharpened, more strength is needed but skill will bring success *(Eccles. 10:10)*.

LEADERS CREATE ATMOSPHERE

*C*elebrate what you
want to see more of.

TOM PETERS

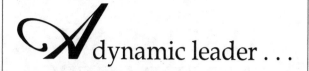

A dynamic leader . . .

*C*ommands respect.

*R*estructures faulty organization.

*E*ducates the team.

*A*cknowledges the potential of others.

*T*akes time for recreation and fun.

*E*nlists other leaders.

*S*olves problems.

LEADERS ARE ENCOURAGERS

*E*veryone thrives on affection and praise.

KEN BLANCHARD

You do not lead by hitting people over the head. That is assault, not leadership.

DWIGHT D. EISENHOWER

*L*eaders never underestimate the power of a note.

Notes should be:

♦ spontaneous

♦ short

♦ sincere

♦ specific

*C*hristians ought to be in the business of building people up. There are too many people in the demolition business today.

NORMAN VINCENT PEALE

*R*emember the difference between a boss and a leader: A boss says, "Go!" A leader says, "Let's go!"

E. M. KELLEY

LEADERS HAVE A
SENSE OF HUMOR

---

*M*ost smiles were
started by another
smile!

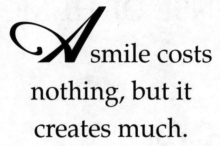

A smile costs
nothing, but it
creates much.

*I*f you're going to
make fun of someone,
start with yourself.

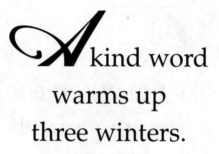

A kind word
warms up
three winters.

CHINESE PROVERB

LEADERS ARE MENTORS

---

*P*eople buy into the leader before they buy into the leader's vision.

JOHN C. MAXWELL

*L*eaders model excellence and quality.
A leader:

   *M*aintains the mission.

   *O*versees the plan.

   *D*evelops more leaders.

   *E*ncourages the heart.

   *L*oves to celebrate.

*M*odeling
is leadership validating itself.

*M*ultiplying
is leadership fashioning its future.

*M*anaging
is leadership conserving its strength.

*M*inistry
is leadership passing on its life.

HAROLD L. LONGENECKER

*L*ead people—not organizations.

BYRON BAGGETT

LEADERS ARE LISTENERS

---

*M*y dear brothers, take note of this: Everyone should be quick to listen, slow to speak and slow to become angry *(James 1:19)*.

*L*istening is the foundation upon which all leadership is developed.

LOUGHLAN SOFIELD

*A*s Jesus and his disciples were on their way, he came to a village where a woman named Martha opened her home to him. She had a sister called Mary, who sat at the Lord's feet listening to what he said. But Martha was distracted by all the preparations that had to be made. She came to him and asked, "Lord, don't you care that my sister has left me to do the work by myself? Tell her to help me!"

"Martha, Martha," the Lord answered, "you are worried and upset about many things, but only one thing is needed. Mary has chosen what is better, and it will not be taken away from her" *(Luke 10:38-42)*.

*Y*ou can learn a lot
by observing.

YOGI BERRA

*T*oday's preparation determines tomorrow's achievements.

ROBERT KLINE

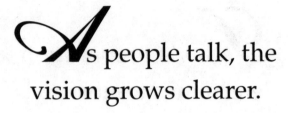

s people talk, the
vision grows clearer.

PETER SENGE

LEADERS VALUE TIME

---

*L*eaders are
proactive and willing
to take a risk.

*T*ips for Time Management

♦ Establish time limits for all meetings.

♦ Return phone calls in time blocks.

♦ Limit daily appointments.

♦ Throw away junk mail.

♦ Prioritize tasks to be done.

*T*he winners in life think constantly in terms of "I can," "I will," and "I am." Losers, on the other hand, concentrate on what they should have done, or what they don't do.

DENNIS WAITLEY

LEADERS ARE CREDIBLE

---

*D*avid shepherded them with integrity of heart; with skillful hands he led them *(Ps. 78:72)*.

*T*he supreme quality
for a leader is
unquestionable
integrity.

CHUCK SWINDOLL

*I*ntegrity is the
crucible of leadership.

*C*haracter and integrity are the cornerstone of business trust.

*J*udge character and ability, not gender.

FREDERICK TALBOTT

A leader has to be a reflection of the soul of the organization.

PHILIP CROSBY

*E*ffective leadership is more than just engaging in action-oriented activities. It is a way of positively influencing others through one's own being.

EDWIN FRIEDMAN

*L*eadership is an action, not a word.

RICHARD COOLEY

*L*eaders call others
to a high standard
of integrity.

LEADERS ARE DECISIVE

---

*D*ecision is the spark that ignites action. Until a decision is made, nothing happens.

WILLARD PETERSON

*L*ove people.

*E*njoy life.

*A*lways involve others.

*D*irect the flow.

*E*xcel in all things.

*R*eady yourself for new challenges.

A great leader takes people where they don't readily want to go, but ought to be.

ROSLYN CARTER

*L*eaders are not smarter than followers —they just think differently.

*T*he quality of a person's life is in direct proportion to their commitment to excellence regardless of their chosen field of endeavor.

VINCE LOMBARDI

*Y*ou are today where your thoughts have brought you. You will be tomorrow where your thoughts take you.

JAMES ALLEN

*H*e Who Knows . . .

He who knows, and knows he knows is wise.

Follow him.

He who knows, and doesn't know he knows is ignorant.

Enlighten him.

He who doesn't know, and doesn't know he doesn't know is a fool.

Avoid him.

He who doesn't know, and knows he does not know is a student.

Teach him.

RUSSIAN PROVERB

LEADERS ARE GOAL-DRIVEN

*S*uccessful people
weave habits of
effectiveness into
their lives.

STEPHEN COVEY

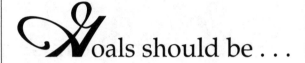

Goals should be . . .

Specific

Measurable

Attainable

Realistic

Time-bound

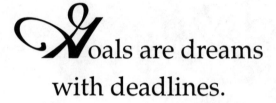

Goals are dreams
with deadlines.

LEADERS ARE
TEAM BUILDERS

---

*T*eamwork is saying,
"OK," instead of,
"It's not my job!"

*T*he best morale exists
when you rarely hear
the word mentioned.
When you hear a lot of
talk about morale, it's
usually very poor.

DWIGHT D. EISENHOWER

*W*hen you ask,
"How are you?"
—mean it!

*C*ompliment your
teammates on a job
well done.

*S*hare a cup of coffee
with a teammate
without being asked.

Ask a teammate's advice on a subject you know nothing about.

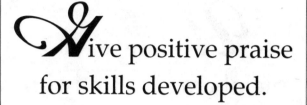

ive positive praise
for skills developed.

*U*pdate team members constantly on win/win situations.

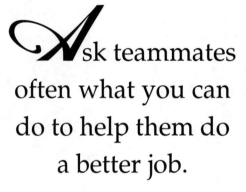

Ask teammates
often what you can
do to help them do
a better job.

*T*eam leadership is remembering the names of your teammates.

*T*eamwork is making new team members feel welcome and glad to be a part of the team!

*R*eview team goals frequently to ensure that they are reasonable.

*P*rovide a learning
environment for team
members.

*C*aring is contagious—
pass it on!

*F*eedback should
be directed to
the full team.

*T*ry reaching consensus. A majority vote does not guarantee validity.

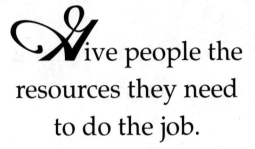

ive people the resources they need to do the job.

*S*tart team meetings
on time.

*S*tate the purpose of
all team meetings.

*S*hare successes with
celebrations.

*C*learly define job
duties, responsibilities,
and priorities.

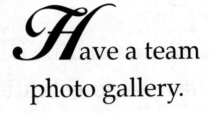

$\mathcal{H}$ave a team photo gallery.

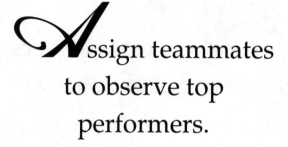

Assign teammates
to observe top
performers.

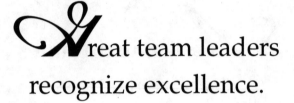

Great team leaders recognize excellence.

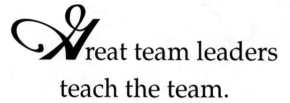

Great team leaders
teach the team.

*T*eam leaders focus
on the goal.

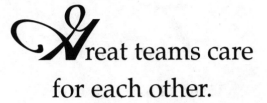

Great teams care
for each other.

*T*eam leaders
understand role
definition.

*T*eam members
recognize the
importance of saying,
"Forgive me."

*T*eam leaders should select teammates who work well with others.

*T*eam leaders who
mentor potential
leaders multiply their
effectiveness.

*T*eam leaders facilitate
good communication by
responding to the
information needs of
an organization.

*G*ood team leaders
seek to understand
what motivates team
members.

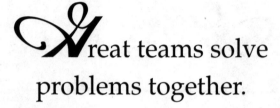

reat teams solve problems together.

*T*eam accountability
is an important essential
to team morale.

*V*alue team members'
differences.

*T*eam leaders know
how to accept praise
and criticism.

$\mathcal{C}$elebrate the
"special days" of
your teammates.

*T*eams that play
together stay together.

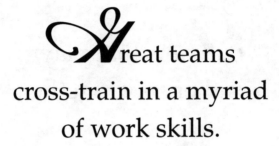

Great teams
cross-train in a myriad
of work skills.

*T*eam leaders are quick to share the success with other teammates!

*P*raise loudly and
blame softly.

*T*eam success and individual success are synonymous.

*T*eamwork involves
listening and
responding.

*T*eam leaders walk
their talk!

LEADERS ARE SPIRITUAL

---

*M*ay the words of my mouth and the meditation of my heart be pleasing in your sight, O LORD, my Rock and my Redeemer *(Ps. 19:14).*

*T*he architecture of leadership, all the theories and guidelines, fall apart without honesty and integrity.

*D*ivorced from ethics, leadership is reduced to management, and politics to mere techniques.

A Leader's Steps to a Closer Relationship with God

1. Establish a daily time for Bible reading and prayer.

2. Find a spiritual mentor to meet with on a regular basis.

3. Read books that reflect the need for intimacy with God.

4. Retreat for 24 hours of meditation, reading, and prayer.

5. Attend church regularly.

*C*onsistency should
be one of the main cogs
in the machinery of
any organized leader.

Godly Leader

- ♦ finds strength by realizing his weaknesses.
- ♦ finds authority by being under authority.
- ♦ finds direction by laying down his own plans.
- ♦ finds vision by seeing the needs of others.
- ♦ finds credibility by being an example.
- ♦ finds loyalty by expressing compassion.
- ♦ finds honor by being faithful.
- ♦ finds greatness by being a servant.

ROY LESSIN

*T*rust, honesty, and integrity are exceedingly important qualities, because they do strongly affect followers.

Guidelines for Successful Leadership

- ◆ Patient in all things.

- ◆ Generous to a fault.

- ◆ Prioritize the schedule.

- ◆ Simplify the process.

- ◆ Love the people.

- ◆ Empower the followers.

- ◆ Never give up!

Other published works
by Dr. Stan Toler include:

*God Has Never Failed Me, But He's Sure
    Scared Me to Death a Few Times*
Essentials to Evangelism
75 Years of Powerful Preaching
Proven Principles of Stewardship
Lessons for Growing Christians
Church Operations Manual
Minister's Little Instruction Book
ABCs of Evangelism
Pastor's Guide to Events and Celebrations
Pastor's Guide to Model Forms and Letters
101 Ways to Grow a Healthy Sunday School
You Might Be a Preacher If . . .